The Library of
E-Commerce and Internet Careers

Careers
as a
Webmaster
Maintaining
the Site

Christopher D. Goranson

The Rosen Publishing Group, Inc.
New York

Published in 2001 by The Rosen Publishing Group, Inc.
29 East 21st Street, New York, NY 10010

Copyright © 2001 by The Rosen Publishing Group, Inc.

First Edition

Library of Congress Cataloging-in-Publication Data

Goranson, Christopher D.
Careers as a webmaster: maintaining the site / Christopher D. Goranson.
    p. cm. — (The library of e-commerce and Internet careers)
Includes bibliographical references and index.
ISBN 0-8239-3419-5 (library binding)
1. Internet—Vocational guidance—Juvenile literature. 2. Webmasters—Juvenile literature. [1. Webmasters—Vocational guidance. 2. Vocational guidance.] I. Title. II. Series.
TK5105.875.I57 G665 2001
005.2'76'02373—dc21

                                           2001000658

Manufactured in the United States of America

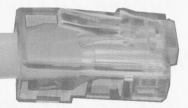

Table of Contents

Introduction

One hundred years from now, when a school teacher begins to explain the phenomenon of the Internet and the exciting events that occurred at the turn of the century, there is no doubt that his or her students will listen intently. One of those stories of the future might just be your own contribution to the Internet! We are living in exciting times. Just as there were individuals who had remarkable stories to tell about the advent of the automobile, electricity, or the Apollo moon landing, we will also have the privilege of sharing our remarkable stories with others. A Webmaster's challenge of working with the fast pace of the Internet is just part of the excitement of our rapidly changing world.

When the Internet first began to seep into the public realm, it was being loosely maintained by groups of scientists, government personnel, teachers, and others. There were few specific job titles, few standards, and very few, if any, classes taught on how to construct a Web page. As the Internet grew, however, people began to become specialized in handling and working with electronic information. And, for those universities or businesses that were the first organizations to create and maintain an Internet presence, there were, of course, people who worked on those Web sites. Later, these computer wizards became known as Webmasters.

The thing to remember about the Internet is that there is plenty of growing room. Chances are that if you are interested in

In the Beginning...

The Internet is expanding at an unbelievable pace and affecting many different areas of our lives. Here are some highlights:

▶ Percentage of words in *Webster's English Dictionary* registered as domain names: 98

▶ Amount spent on advertising by dot-com companies in 1999, in billions of dollars: 3.1

▶ Percentage of full-time, four-year college students in the United States who use the Internet: 90

designing Web sites, you will be able to find a good fit for your abilities!

Just as the scope of the Internet increases, so does Internet business. E-commerce, buying and selling products and services electronically, is among the most rapidly growing fields in the world, globally accounting for nearly $132 billion in 2000. And that isn't just established merchants with recognizable names such as Barnes & Noble; sometimes it's a mom-and-pop business in your own neighborhood.

"The e-commerce medium will offer unmatched potential to reach mass-market consumers conveniently, competitively, and creatively."

—Steve Case, chairman and CEO, America Online

The power of e-commerce is in the hands of the people. Consumers now have more products, services, and information in their hands than they ever had before. Search engines allow consumers to locate products from around the world and carry out transactions with the click of a mouse. According to many, allowing people to buy what they want when they want it is the single-biggest driving force behind the growth of the e-commerce market.

Masters of the Internet Universe

WHERE DID WEBMASTERS BEGIN?

When the Internet was first popularized, people who had the most interest or knowledge about maintaining an HTML (hypertext markup language) document maintained Web pages. There were no fancy animated intros, no Java, and hardly any dynamic content in Web sites at all. The early sites were usually very simple, often merely text written in basic HTML with minimal graphics. As you know, the Internet rapidly changed. In just a few years, the Web has gone from simple content-driven sites to sites that are more complex, dynamic, and interactive.

The primary people responsible for creating the sites that changed the Internet became known as Webmasters. Webmasters are generally known as

Webmasters use a variety of different hardware and software tools in addition to their creativity.

people who maintain, and sometimes create, Web sites. Think of a Webmaster's job as the equivalent of an editor's job when he or she revises a book, only the Webmaster is working on an electronic file, and the Web site is like an online book. It can inform people about a school, an organization, or a company. Chances are your school already has a Web site maintained by a Webmaster.

Webmasters are often people who have some sort of computer background, but that isn't always the case. Often, Webmasters started out when they were your age or younger, simply by experimenting on computers in their spare time. Many never thought that they would develop a career as a Webmaster; after all, not too long ago, there was hardly a need for so many savvy computer specialists! Some Webmasters may have a background in art or graphic design, which makes them particularly good at deciding how each Web site should look and what the visitor should experience when they visit. These people are usually known as Web designers, and we will refer to them later in this book. Many have a solid understanding of computer language programming, such as HTML, Java, and now JavaScript, which makes it easier for them to understand difficult Web programming.

Today, there are many classes offered for people who are interested in becoming Webmasters. Some of these classes are very basic and simply introduce beginners to the Web. Others are advanced and teach people how to program dynamic sites containing animations, graphics, security systems, and integrated bulletin boards and chat rooms. Sites may also contain sound or video files, and they may be connected to a database or a network of other computers.

People often assume that because the Internet relies so heavily on computers, anyone who works on the Internet must also be computer savvy. While this may be the case for specific types of work, such as computer programming, the Internet is more like a community of jobs. There are many different types of careers that require assorted skills. Artists, musicians, managers, and creative individuals have all found a home on the Internet, yet many of them are not programmers.

In the Internet world, what looked spectacular a few months ago may now seem rather average. That's an important idea to keep in mind. Because the Web continues to change at such a rapid pace, Webmasters and developers must change with it. This gives you, an aspiring Webmaster with a fresh outlook, the perfect opportunity to jump in! After all, when a new programming language or Web tool becomes available, you'll be starting at the same place as someone who has been developing Web sites for years. And while that person might have an advantage because of his or her experience in other areas, you'll both be learning something new. In a year's time, it's quite possible that you'll quickly become a specialist in the latest form of software or language.

Some of the best Flash (a popular animation program) designers are under the age of twenty. This should tell you something. Just like you, the Web is young, and it is built with even younger tools. One of the best ways to begin learning about the Internet is to get involved. This book will help you get your own Web site up and running without spending a penny. Now, let's get started!

BUSINESS FROM THE STREET TO THE NET: WHAT'S THE DIFFERENCE?

As businesses turn more and more to the Internet—going from brick-and-mortar (physical store) to click-and-mortar (online store)—so do the people who work in traditional businesses. During the dot-com heyday in the late 1990s and the early part of the new millennium, it was not uncommon to see CEOs and others from traditional businesses make the jump to the Internet. Business is business, though, and although the Internet revolution forced people to reconsider how things were done, these changes certainly did not replace traditional business practices. Because of this, there was an obvious need for business experts to become a part of the Internet world.

Today, leaders and a board of directors who have extensive business experience manage most large

1. **Think of your Web page as your product catalog**. Essentially, an e-commerce Web site is nothing more than an exclusive, sometimes interactive, catalog. The difference when you shop online, however, is that a Web page is marketed to be an "experience." Online businesses must now create small communities within the Internet where people feel as if they "belong," and buying the products offered on the site makes them feel like participants in the community they love.

2. **Create a place to store purchases**. Just like in a retail store, e-commerce Web sites have a "shopping cart" service to keep track of purchases.

3. **Offer payment options**. While you may not be equipped to take and store credit card information over a secure server, you do have other options, such as accepting standard check or money orders, or utilizing services like e-cash. This is an online service that allows users to pass "virtual" money from points A to B anonymously. Plus, there are plenty of methods to accept credit card payments by setting up your e-commerce site through an established resource, such as eBay.com—the famed auction community that uses BillPoint or PayPal—both money-sending services that allow consumers to pay for products using their checking accounts. Think of these services as "virtual banks" that

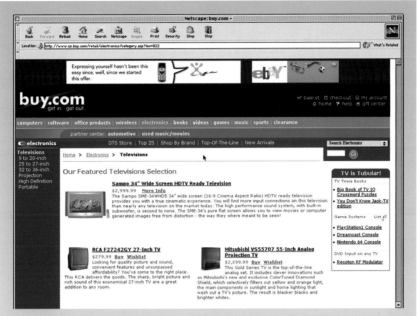

Buy.com offers the traditional features of an e-commerce site, such as detailed product descriptions.

allow people to e-mail you money. These services are easy, secure, and nearly instant.

4. **Order fulfillment**. Before you offer products for sale online, make certain that you can deliver what you promise. If, for instance, you are creating a Web site that features T-shirts, make sure that you have enough inventory to meet your expected demand.

5. **The customer is always right**. Well, maybe not always, but this is what you want him or her to think. Offer the best customer service that you possibly can. Nowadays, there are many free, downloadable "perks" to offer customers. A few standard tools that should be available to customers are e-mail notification and a listing of customer service FAQs (frequently asked questions), such as "What is your return policy?"

dot-coms. And, while actual purchases may take place electronically instead of in an actual store, there are still many steps surrounding the sale that have not changed. For instance, let's say that you visited a site on the Internet and bought a new DVD movie. What's the difference between buying the movie on the Internet versus buying it from a store? Well, when you get right down to it, not much. For nearly every Internet purchase, you must use a credit card. You can also use a credit card at your local store. When ordering from the Internet, you will probably have to wait at least a couple of days to get the DVD delivered to your home. Someone needs to take the order and process it, someone else has to package it, and yet another person has to mail it to your door. If you bought the DVD from your local video store, you may be able to walk out with it in your hand if the store happens to have it in stock. But, let's say that it's a movie that hasn't been released in large volumes, or that it's a new release your store recently sold out of. Just like your Internet purchase, the neighborhood store now will have to place the order for you, someone will have to package it, and another person will have to mail it to the store so you can pick it up. As you can see, there's not really a great deal of difference other than how the DVD was purchased. In many ways, this is how the Internet has affected businesses. It allows more options for consumers than they would get in a physical store. In fact, you might be surprised to learn just how easy it is to create an e-commerce Web site that performs many of the same functions as any other site, including the one where you made that DVD purchase.

The term "e-commerce" basically means buying or selling products or services through an online medium. For example, if you created a Web page with several products pictured on it, and offered nothing more than a description of your inventory, pricing, and contact information, then you have created an e-commerce Web site. Now, if someone decided to buy one of your products, e-mailed you, and then sent you a check, you have completed an e-commerce transaction.

At this point, you might be wondering what it takes to be an effective e-commerce Webmaster. There is one basic principle to remember if you are considering a Webmaster's job: It is a position that is changing dramatically so you should get involved now. However, the e-commerce market is still being tested, and lessons are still being learned.

Some Webmasters may work at home in their bathrobes, but for many, the job requires meetings, travel, and being accessible twenty-four hours a day to fix any technical problems that might arise with the site.

Not Your Ordinary Workday

*M*arvin likes his lifestyle. He rolls out of bed, puts on his bunny slippers, and goes to work with a toothbrush still in his mouth. Marvin likes the freedom of working from home, even though it often turns into longer hours than he would have otherwise spent at the office. He values being able to finish work without many distractions, and working at home gives him an opportunity to spend more time with his four-year-old son.

Webmasters don't always wake up and go right to work. But there are a good number of Webmasters who simply do just that: They roll out of bed, make some coffee, pick up the newspaper, and wander into the next room—their "office." Ah, yes, the charmed life of a Webmaster. Never before has it been so easy to join a conference call in your bathrobe.

The Webmaster's lifestyle has been a trend lately. More and more, people that are joining the workforce are not actually working in the office, but at home. Telecommuting, otherwise known as working at a different location than the one where your coworkers are, is becoming more popular than ever. It's not something reserved just for Webmasters either. People are working from home in record numbers.

As the economy and the companies contributing to it become global, it becomes more difficult to maintain branch offices in new territories. Sometimes it is much more cost-effective to let someone simply work out of his or her home, or out of a mobile office, than to set up a new branch location and a full support staff. Twenty-four-hour copy centers, cell phones, portable computers, and fax machines have made being a traveling business warrior that much easier. There isn't much administrative work that can't be done at home these days.

The Internet has unearthed a rather unique working arrangement. Because people are connected worldwide through the Internet, and because you can tell a customer in England to look at your business's Web site so he or she will see it just as you do, distance does not play such a role in the business world as it once did. Many employers do prefer to have Webmasters working at their on-site locations, however, especially if the site is rapidly changing and frequently updated.

Think of it this way: If you could go to school from your room, wouldn't you? Let's say that instead of waking up in the morning and having to get ready for school, you could simply roll out of bed, walk into the next room, and begin going to class whenever you were ready, via your computer. It sounds tempting, doesn't it? This isn't to say a Webmaster's work is necessarily easy, but it is tempting to have a work-at-home arrangement with employers. However, working from home is not for everybody. Some people have a hard time separating their professional lives from their personal lives.

Christina Nippert-Eng, an associate professor of sociology at the Illinois Institute of Technology in Chicago, says there are some things you should consider before deciding to work from home. Because some people are better than others at separating work from their regular lives, it is important to make sure that the company you work with will also support this separation. She says there are those who are great at separating work from home life, and they are called "integrators." The workers at the other end of the spectrum are called "segmenters," individuals who would rather keep their personal lives completely separate from anything work-related. Keep these ideas in mind before taking the plunge away from the office.

Interview Your Boss

If you do work from home, you should try to establish independent measures to make sure that you will be judged on equal grounds with your peers as much as possible.

Improve Your Communication Skills

Working from a remote location can lead to miscommunications, and careless e-mail writing can lead to trouble. There's a difference between "Could you forward this report on to Jill please?" and "Give this to Jill." Simple, yet true.

Privacy Is a Concern

Just because you are working from a computer in your bedroom doesn't mean that your company gives up the right to read your e-mail. It's easy to blur the lines when working at home, but don't forget that e-mail and telephone policies are likely the same whether in a cubicle or in a bedroom.

As with any career, you need to take into consideration not only what you are going to do, but where you are going to do it. The Internet changes the way we think about the workplace and about business, for better or for worse.

FREELANCERS AND THE INTERNET

Lindsay attended school full-time and needed a good job to earn money for tuition. Because she had a varied schedule and couldn't commit to a regular nine-to-five position, she decided to try her hand at the freelance market. She had exceptional talent as a photographer, knew HTML, and had already won a number of awards for her work, so Lindsay signed up with Guru.com (www.guru.com), a Web site that profiles freelance talent and job opportunities. After several weeks, she was contacted by a local grassroots newspaper that needed help building its Web site. It wasn't that Lindsay planned to become a photographer or a Webmaster, but the freelance position helped her pay for school and keep her schedule flexible.

Sites such as Guru.com offer opportunities for freelance work, which is a good way to gain experience working with Web pages and other Web designers.

Freelancers are a growing population of individuals who specialize in picking up short-term contracts when a company needs a specific talent for a limited time. For example, a Java freelancer might be hired because of his or her specific programming knowledge, but perhaps the company needs an employee only for a few weeks. In such a case, it would not make much sense to hire a full-time person for the job. Freelancers are becoming an increasingly popular option for companies that need temporary, but often high-caliber, talent.

Becoming a Successful
Webmaster: Attitude Is Everything!

As we discussed in chapter 1, many successful Webmasters are creative people. In this chapter, we're going to look at some ways that you can help yourself become a successful Webmaster right now!

It's very important to keep in mind that in the Internet universe, you must consistently learn about the latest advancements in technology. This is extremely important because the Internet changes so rapidly. Obviously, the best way to do this is by getting involved now.

A funny thing seems to happen to people when they get involved with computer technology. After a while, they seem to think that they know everything. Perhaps this is because they do know a great deal, often more than the people they meet, or they think that no one else can learn what they know. After working in an area that many people find difficult to understand or are afraid of trying to learn, it's easy for people to begin thinking of themselves as extremely witty and intelligent creatures who have some superhuman power. Don't let this happen to you! It's extremely easy to believe that you know much more than you really do, and this can be dangerous. This attitude could lead you to make unwise decisions and may also make it extremely easy for someone else to notice that you really don't know as much as you think you do.

Remember to stay humble in your new profession. Use your knowledge to help others understand what you are doing. What could be a better reward than that? You should never reach a point where you know everything about anything, especially if you choose a career as a Webmaster. Remember, you had to learn how to operate a mouse and keyboard like everyone else. Knowledge is something that is learned one step at a time.

KEYS TO SUCCESS: CASE STUDIES

It's hard to explain the variety of opportunities waiting on the Internet without some good examples. Whether you become a Webmaster yourself or work closely with one, chances are your experiences may be very unique. This chapter presents two very different case studies, but both deal with individuals who are heavily involved with the Internet.

Case Study No. 1: Matt

Yes, that's right. MTV's *Real World New Orleans* cast member Matt is a Web developer. But Matt didn't get his start by studying Web design in school. Or, at least, not directly. As is the case with many Web designers and Webmasters, many times people have fallen into their current careers. There once was a time when few people were willing to actually pay someone to maintain a

"Pay attention and try to catch the next big tech wave."
—Matt, MTV *Real World* cast member

Some of Matt's Favorite Web Sites

www.threeoh.com
www.blackhand.com
And, of course, his own site, www.supa-fly.com

Web Design Tools Matt Uses

Adobe Photoshop and other tools from the Adobe product line (www.adobe.com).

Web site, and it certainly wasn't an activity that some-one could consider a career. Web-related positions have evolved significantly since then, and Matt's story is a common one that helps explain how many people first became Webmasters.

Matt's first experiences with the Internet were in 1995 when he was a college student. Interestingly enough, the first Web site he remembers visiting was MTV.com. He remembers thinking it needed some serious reorganization! As was the case at the time, careers for Webmasters and Web developers hadn't fully evolved, so many sites were the product of people simply throwing things together and experimenting.

Matt originally went to school for graphic design and eventually ended up drifting into the World Wide Web. During the summer of 1999, Matt dove into the Internet headfirst. He says he learned every-thing by simply "watching the best." He identified leading Web designers and developers, and started to notice trends and ideas evolving and emerging from this core group. Looking back, Matt says that his drawing and painting classes were the most helpful when learning how to design Web pages. He also describes the Internet as an "accessible library of resources at your fingertips."

Matt identified several advantages that he felt younger generations would have when it came to building careers as Webmasters: "The software just keeps getting better and better. As the entire Web environment changes, the technologies surrounding the Web become better and more specialized.

"As the Web evolves, so will the relationship between television and the Internet. Online and interactive television will become a reality. More movies will be released on and for the Internet. More grassroots films, music, and other Internet-capable media will gain in popularity because of the Internet and the resources made available by the Internet."

Finally, Matt suggests up-and-coming Webmasters use their imaginations. "Pay attention and try to catch the next big tech wave. Catch the next one!" Like many things in life, the Web is influenced by trends. If you compare cutting-edge Web sites today to sites created just two years ago, you'd notice a big difference in design. That is because the Web, like many media outlets, goes through a number of phases as it becomes more developed. Just like clothing, Web design goes in and out of style. You can be certain that if, in ten years, you were attempting to run your business from a site that had been developed today, it would look as strange as if you dug out some decade-old clothing and went to class.

Case Study No. 2: Dr. Tai-Dan Hsu, G*Barter.com, Inc.

Dr. Hsu is the president and CEO of G*Barter.com (www.gbarter.com), a new Web site that focuses on trading goods and services to sell antiques and collectibles. G*Barter.com is unique because it allows members to exchange their items with other members and get credit for their exchanges, which they can later apply toward items they want. Trading occurs by using "barter dollars," which are credits that represent an item's value. The advantage to the site as compared to many other barter sites is that a member doesn't have to trade with only one member at a time—what's known as a one-to-one trade. (Older barter sites required you to find something you wanted from another member, but in order for that member to want to trade with you, he or she had to want something that you were trading—sometimes a difficult prospect.) Because Dr. Hsu realized this difficulty (and that the items had to be of similar value to be fair), he created a site where people could exchange items for credits, which could be used later to swap for a different member's items.

Dr. Hsu was relatively new to the Internet world when he first embarked on G*Barter, but he had developed a successful career running a traditional brick-and-mortar company. Because of his experience, Dr. Hsu makes some interesting observations about switching over to the Net.

He views the Internet as a virtual library, with information on just about everything you could imagine. However, he says, this isn't always a good thing. Because of the absurd amount of material that is available to anyone with a computer, he says students need to develop skills to sift through information to pick out useful jewels.

How Techies Spend Their Days

"The Internet creates the opportunity for young people to be more creative"
—**Dr. Hsu, president and CEO of G*Barter.com**

Dr. Hsu's Favorite Web Site
www.ebay.com

How He Sums Up His Advice
"Don't be afraid!"

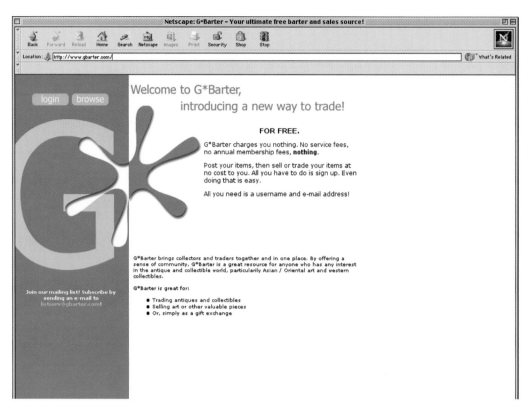

G*Barter.com enables users to trade with each other and get credit for their exchanges, which can be applied toward items they want in the future.

When Dr. Hsu was developing the framework behind the ideas that would later become G*Barter.com, he realized that he would be successful only if he was able to identify something people wanted, have a creative and effective way to deliver it, and be able to make money from the exchange. He also mentioned that even if he wasn't able to make money, he would be content to share his idea with the world and be encouraged by the fact that people found what he created useful.

According to Dr. Hsu, today's teens will have a distinct advantage on the Internet. He believes that they can be much more creative than the established members of the business community. Also, because of the inexpensive methods available to share that creativity on the Web, they can more readily share their ideas with the world and expose their creativity, letting it blossom and grow. "The Internet creates the opportunity for young people to be more creative."

FROM THE INSIDE OUT: ANATOMY OF AN E-COMMERCE WEB SITE

Now that you have learned the basics, let's examine them a bit more closely. Everyone understands that there are many elements to consider when you're building and designing the perfect Web site, but what makes designing an e-commerce Web site even more of a challenge? This question may have several basic answers, including the following: clearly showing your product; knowing your purpose and your audience; basic, easy-to-understand navigation; interesting, error-free editorial content; established customer loyalty and trust; and customer feedback. Also, while it might be your goal to add every bell and whistle that you can find to your page, consider

Since computer monitors display images at a resolution of 72 dpi, most images posted on the Web are scanned at this resolution. Magazines and books use images with 300 dpi resolution.

that each person viewing it (each potential customer) may not be equipped with a computer fast enough to download the toys. Many, many big companies have fallen into this trap: They hire an expensive freelance Web team to build a mega-site, only to find that customers really want to view only a product photo, read a short description, and punch in a credit card number. The video clip and animation banner ad really did nothing to entertain or engage the customer. And, if these additions keep the site from loading quickly, you risk losing that sale. E-commerce can be tricky.

A word about product photography: Because your Web customer cannot examine the items that you are selling, you need to capture his or her interest with a photograph. Make sure that the final image is cropped, clear, and flattering. Use the best possible image that you can. (Ultimately, everyone on the Web is viewing any imagery at 72 dpi [dots per inch], so using a poor-quality photograph with a high-quality scanner will get you nowhere.)

Understanding your audience is a bit more complicated. Of course, you won't have focus groups to tell you who is most likely to view your site, but if you do know your product (and you should), you will most likely know a lot about your customers. Say, for example, you are selling skateboards. Since you probably know the skate scene in your area, think about all the interests of your potential customers. Where do they skate? What are their needs while skating? Do they listen to music while they skate? Do they wear helmets or other safety equipment? If you think about every aspect surrounding your customers' interests, it will make it much easier to anticipate how you should construct your Web site and what you should (and shouldn't) include.

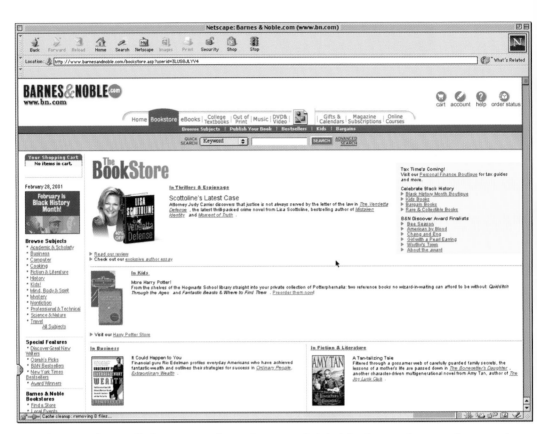

Web sites that sell things, such as Barnes & Noble (www.bn.com), must be well designed and composed, reliable, and easy for customers to navigate.

Now, here are some thoughts about navigation. Navigation refers to how your customers move around your Web site. The best idea for easy navigation is to have clearly marked paths or choices for viewers to make while they are browsing your site. For instance, you wouldn't want your customer to point and click his or her way to an error message. Broken links, or links that lead to error messages, can be discouraging to anyone. Keep your navigation as simple as possible while still including some of the basics, such as "escape" links on the top and bottom of every page.

The editorial content of your site is as important as the graphics. Just like you want the best possible photography to show off your wares, you also want to write about them in a good, clean style that is correct. People judge Web sites according to their accuracy. There is no room for errors in spelling, punctuation, grammar, or readability. Grab a friend, a parent, or a teacher to go over your work and use the spell-checker. Consider the editorial content of your site as another way to entertain your viewers. Make them laugh. Give them an interesting story, a tidbit of knowledge, or a thoughtful quote. Hopefully, if you are able to capture your audience's imagination, they will return and eventually buy.

If you concern yourself with the details, customers will follow. Write a mission statement for your site, and if you request information from your customers, tell them how you are going to use it. Write a privacy policy that outlines your intentions. Be aware of the promises that you make, and, last but not least, make sure you have enough inventory to fill your needs!

Preparing Today for a Career Tomorrow

I f you're serious about becoming involved in the Internet, there is no better time to begin than now.

There are a number of skills that make a good Webmaster: creativity, organizational and artistic ability, and vision are just a few. Where do you think you could learn such skills? College, perhaps? Maybe art school? Well, those places can certainly help, but chances are you already have some of these abilities. The point is that there is nothing stopping you from becoming a Webmaster *right now*. While taking classes in Web design and development will help, chances are, if you're going to be a good Web designer, you probably already are. Never underestimate creativity—it is the lifeblood behind the Web. Want proof? Just look at how quickly Web sites change! What looks chic and hip one year can quickly look bland and generic the next. The Web is run on

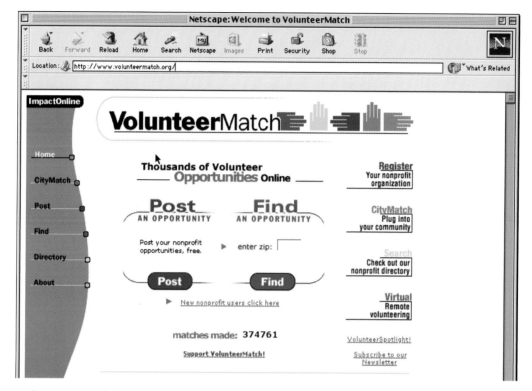

Web sites such as VolunteerMatch (www.volunteermatch.org) offer many opportunities for new Webmasters to gain Web design experience and make money.

ideas, and there is no reason to think that you might not have the next great one!

GREAT PLACES TO START

Many schools have invested time and effort to build a presence on the Internet. Check around and see if there are any opportunities for interns or special classes for students who want to learn about Web design. Your computer lab may also have Web editing software, giving you an opportunity to learn advanced computer programs during high school.

Helpful Career Sites

www.volunteermatch.org
This Web site matches your skills and available time with those who need your help. Connections made here and through any volunteer work can lead to many opportunities.

www.guru.com
This Web site is dedicated to the freelance community and offers a number of ways to get started. The site includes resources for the independent professional, and you can browse the job listings to see if there are any good opportunities for your skill level.

www.w3schools.com
This Web site offers tutorial resources for Webmasters and developers alike. It's a terrific place to stop whenever you have a Web design question.

Webmasters must keep up with changing technologies, so you may have to study or take classes to increase your knowledge.

If not, there are a number of online resources available for anyone willing to spend a little time to learn. You may also be able to find a nonprofit organization that will provide you with an opportunity to practice your Webmaster skills by working on a Web site.

The Web also offers a number of ways to learn through online communities where you can form friendships, create business alliances, learn from others, and interact as if you had a huge group of supporters to keep you on track.

Build It and They Will Surf

Do you want to build your own Web site? Do you want to become the Webmaster of your *own* domain? Here are several software programs to help you get started.

STEP 1: THE WEB PAGE EDITOR

It used to be that you had to learn HTML to create a Web page. Today, however, you can create Web sites with no programming skills and, better yet, no money. A number of resources exist on the Internet that can help connect you with W.Y.S.I.W.Y.G. (What You See Is What You Get) editors, many of which are specifically built to help beginners construct their first Web pages. Netscape Communicator (www.netscape.com) includes an editor, called Composer, along with its more popular browser. Microsoft (www.microsoft.com)

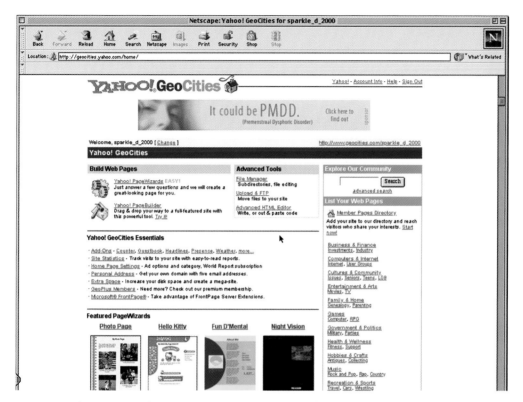

Many Web sites, such as Yahoo!GeoCities, offer free and low-cost Web editors and other software that will help you build your first Web site.

now provides a simpler version of its more robust HTML editor, FrontPage 2000, in FrontPage Express. Both are suitable for beginners. FrontPage 2000 includes a number of prebuilt templates to help you get a site up and running in no time. Evrsoft.com provides a free HTML editor called First Page and includes free JavaScripts and other features to help you excel quickly. (This is a more advanced editor and does require some knowledge of HTML, but it will be a nice complement to other programs after you have learned the basics.)

STEP 2: FINDING A HOST

GeoCities (www.geocities.com) and Angelfire (www.angelfire.com) include not only free editors and other utilities for creating a Web site but also offer free hosting. It's not as good as having your own domain hosted (often using a free Web host means limitations in space and service), but if you want to go that route you can find affordable Web hosting for around $9.95 per month and up. The Web hosting market seems to become increasingly competitive every day, so do some shopping around before you make any commitment. A good place to begin is the Web Host Directory (www.webhostdir.com), which rates Web hosting companies according to a number of criteria, including price, accessibility, and site-building tools.

If you want to use a professional Web hosting company for your site, you'll have to register your domain name. To check on available names, use a service like Network Solutions (www.networksolutions.com). Most will charge about $35 per year to register your domain name with InterNIC, but this price has dropped as more competitors flood the market. If you want a good in-between solution, you can register your domain name and then have it redirected to your free host using a service like Namesecure (www.namesecure.com).

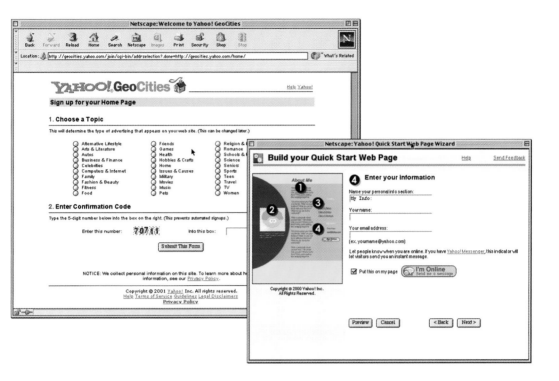

Many Web sites offer free or affordable Web hosting, but these are usually supported by mandatory advertising that may appear on your site.

STEP 3: WORKING ON THE SITE

Of course, you'll want to find out how you can make your Web site better and attract more visitors, right? Well, lucky for you, there are a number of sites out there that can help you get started. For graphics, check out ArtToday.com and Clipart.com, and for great design ideas, visit Zeldman.com. Want to add some more pizzazz to those Web sites? Check out MapBlast.com, a site that allows you to attach fully browseable maps to your site. A number of other Web sites provide free, streaming news, covering everything from politics to sports to weather and celebrity gossip.

In general, there are five major steps to take into consideration when building your site. To make the visualization process easier, think of it in terms of building a robot.

1. Content: What you want the robot to do

2. Site Architecture: The skeleton of the robot

3. Site Implementation and Population: The guts of the robot

4. Graphic Design: The skin of the robot

5. Site Maintenance: Making sure that your robot does what you tell it to, stays well, and does not forget any information

This may be sort of a strange approach to explaining how to build a Web site, but a site is much more than just a few pages. There should be a central idea behind how it is designed. This philosophy helps to shape the experience for your visitor, and if the experience is a good one, filled with interesting and useful information, your site is likely to receive more "hits" from people who have surfed on over.

First, you need to come up with what you want the Web site to do. What is the purpose of your site? Think like a reporter. Ask yourself, who or what is the site for? Second, you need to think about and develop a way for all of the pages to link together, sort of like assembling a puzzle. A Web site isn't really a good Web site unless you have created an interesting environment for people to experience— that's where populating it with information and graphics comes in. Finally, your site is only as good as it works. If you are running a site that provides your visitors with tons of information, but they still can't find what they surfed over for, chances are they won't return. As time goes on, you will also need to update and improve both the content and the appearance of your site to keep it current.

EXTRA CREDIT

Want to go the extra mile and make an e-commerce site? Can you believe you can do that for free, too? FreeMerchant (www.freemerchant.com) provides a way to host your online Web site, calculates shipping and handling costs, and contains other free software tools for creating invoices, accepting credit cards, and creating auction listings for things that you have in stock. Now, let's get down to business!

Many companies offer basic e-commerce tools to get you started. (Yahoo Store allows its customers to set up a virtual storefront with complete services that help them process orders and ship items anywhere from $100 per month.) These e-commerce services are called "turnkey solutions," which means that your virtual storefront will have a sort of virtual manager who will help keep the books and handle the accounts. Check out sites like Just Web It! (www.justwebit.com) that offer plenty of services, from Web hosting to "shopping cart" functions to tacking on credit card fulfillment functions to an existing site. Another option is CafePress (www.cafepress.com), a just-add-product type of site that has served hundreds who want to make an e-commerce site for custom T-shirts, coffee mugs, or almost any handmade craft under the sun.

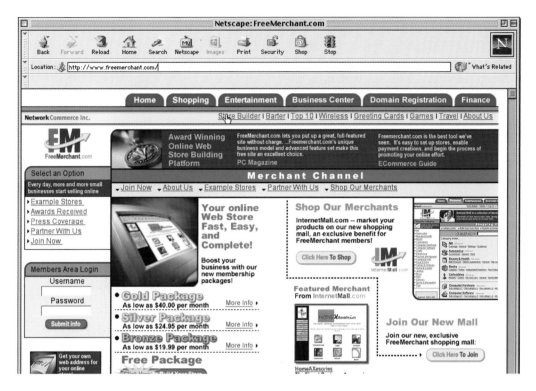

If you want to build an e-business, sites such as FreeMerchant offer tools to help you with business and administrative tasks.

Other handy e-commerce software tools that are available for purchase are NetObjects Fusion, iCat Commerce Online, and IBM HotMedia.

You can be certain that you merely have to walk to any downtown in America to find more than a few businesses that want to grab a piece of virtual storefront on the World Wide Web. They may need someone like you to help get them started.

Let's say that you have a prospective client. Joe, the owner of the local hardware store, wants you to create his Web page. It's important to take inventory of the facts. Do you need to write a mission statement? Maybe Joe's site will require an e-mail link so his customers can keep in touch. What type of pages should you link to the site you have created? Perhaps there is a popular Web site that offers simple home-building plans or instructions for assembling home furnishings. There are many things to consider, especially when you are creating a Web page for a business. Begin by creating a small catalog of the most popular items in stock. For instance, if Joe's Hardware sells unusual switch plates, maybe you want to feature them as a part of your online catalog. Start small and build slowly.

If you're selling items on your site, what have you offered your customers in terms of security? For instance, customers will not want to offer any personal information, such as credit card numbers, unless your site is connected to a secure server. What this means is that whatever information is sent back and forth from your customer to you is encrypted, or scrambled, in a way that nobody can read. (That is, until it reaches its destination and is interpreted.) Most e-tailers now offer connection services via secure servers. Each Web site must disclose this information to its customers. On the other hand, e-mail messages are not secure. If you are not using a secure server to transfer information, then you must explain this to your customers beforehand.

THINGS TO CONSIDER FOR THE FUTURE

For some time now, it has been suggested that we are in the middle of the transition from the Industrial Age to the Information Age. Information is becoming the sought-after commodity of the present and future, replacing machines and products, according to some.

In the Industrial Age and through the 1980s, the idea that an employee entered into a sort of contract with his or her employer was taken for granted. The employee offered loyalty and dedication to one company, and, in turn, that company offered job security and plenty of extra benefits. The idea of leaving a great company to pursue a risky endeavor with a smaller, lesser-known business (much less pursuing the idea of creating a new business) was considered very risky, perhaps crazy, by some.

However, things appear to be changing. Today, employees are less likely to stick it out with one company for life, and even the old stalwarts of the

Industrial Age are being forced to readjust and reform old business practices to keep up with their younger, and perhaps more aggressive, business counterparts. The number of positions filled by temporary-staffing companies grew from 1.35 million to 3.23 million between 1988 and 1998. This was the fastest employment growth of any sector. Today, temporary workers, part-time workers, and independent contractors account for nearly 25 percent of the workforce. Those numbers can be much higher in the high-tech arena.

THE INTERNET BOOM

How will the Internet change the way we live and work? There is little doubt that the Internet is having a profound effect on the way in which business is conducted. The future is certainly bright for anyone who wants to take advantage of the tools and opportunities of tomorrow. As someone just starting to plan for your future, you have the unique ability to position yourself to achieve fantastic career goals. By choosing to become involved in opportunities now, and taking classes that further promote your skills and ideas, you can take advantage of the wide number of possibilities that are now brought right to your front door by the Internet.

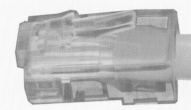

Glossary

address   The unique identifier you need to either access a Web site or to send e-mail.

browser/Web browser   A software program that allows you to surf the Web. Netscape Navigator and Internet Explorer are currently the most popular Web browsers. The very first Web browsers allowed only the viewing of text.

domain name   A unique name that identifies an Internet site. A domain name points to one specific server, while this server may host many domain names. For example, the "www" in a Web site address points to the server, and "yahoo.com" is a domain name.

dot-com   Usually refers to a company that performs the majority or all of its services through an online presence.

e-mail   Electronic mail; a message, usually text, transmitted over the Internet and sent from one person to another, or to a group of people. MIME formatted e-mail messages can send HTML, basically sending a customized Web page instead of text.

FTP (file transfer protocol)   In relation to a Web site, FTP is a method for publishing a Web site from one computer to another. A Webmaster may develop and test the site on her or his own machine and then later move it to the Web server.

hit   A single request from a browser to a server. Because separate downloads of multiple graphics on one Web page are sometimes counted as multiple hits, they are not always a very good gauge of a Web site's popularity.

home page   A home page can refer to either the main page, an entry page for a Web site, or the entire Web site. In general, a user can navigate to all other areas of a site from a home page. A home page can be one page or thousands of pages tied together through links.

host   The server on which a Web site is stored. A Web hosting company will store a number of Web sites on multiple machines connected to the Internet by very fast connections.

HTML (hypertext markup language)   The coding language used to create hypertext documents to be read on the World Wide Web. HTML can be very basic: <B> is an HTML command to make text bold, for example. DHTML (dynamic HTML) can be much more complex and allow for a number of effects.

HTTP (hypertext transfer protocol)   World Wide Web protocol for moving hypertext (HTML) files across the Internet.

hyperlink   A highlighted word or graphic (often image maps) placed within a hypertext document (Web page). When a user clicks on a hyperlink, he or she is moved to another location on the Web.

Internet   The Internet is a network of connected machines that supports multiple users to access networked resources. The Web on the other hand, is a collection of pages or documents written in HTML.

IP (Internet protocol)   The rules that provide basic Internet functions and the method by which computers know how to find each other.

ISP (Internet service provider)   An ISP can provide you with access to the Internet. ISP may also refer to a company that hosts your Web site. For example, EarthLink is an ISP.

Java   A high-level, platform-independent programming language created by Sun Microsystems. Java is a general programming language, but it is well-suited for developing Web pages.

JavaScript   JavaScripts are often small pieces of code that can be inserted into HTML documents to perform more complicated tasks.

JPEG (joint photographic experts group) Image compression standard, optimized for full-color digital images. Photographs are often converted into a JPEG format because of the higher quality resolution it provides.

link   Generally refers to a connection from one Web page to another. A link often refers to a word or series of words, often highlighted in blue and underlined. Images may also be links.

Navigator   Web browser from Netscape.

page/Web page   One single document on the Web.

portal   A Web site that usually offers large amounts of information, with search options and many other free services.

search engine   Web site that collects and provides other resources found on the Web based on information provided by the user. Each search engine collects information differently, which makes it more difficult for Webmasters to predict how popular their site is.

surfing   Browsing the Web; usually refers to someone not looking for anything in particular—like taking a stroll through the World Wide Web and seeing the "sites."

Webmaster   A person or group of people responsible for the design, implementation, management, and maintenance of a Web site. Responsibilities can include the fields of network configuration, interface, graphic design, software development, business strategy, writing, marketing, and project management.

World Wide Web   An Internet client-server system to distribute information, based on the hypertext transfer protocol (HTTP). Also known as WWW, W3, or simply the Web. Created at CERN in Geneva, Switzerland, in 1991 by Dr. Tim Berners-Lee.

W.Y.S.I.W.Y.G. (What You See Is What You Get); acronym that refers to programs that allow you to edit a Web page using the HTML format.

For More Information

CNET
http://www.cnet.com
From job hunting and product reviews to the most
popular downloads, CNET is your one-stop-shop for
everything Internet- and computer-related.

Search Engine Watch
http://www.searchenginewatch.com
You can't tell them about it if they can't find you!
This site explains what to do to get picked up by
the top search engines and directories.

Use It
http://www.useit.com
What makes a truly great Web site? Jakob Nielsen's
tell-all.

Webreference
http://www.webreference.com
Tons and tons of information for Webmasters.

Webtechniques
http://www.webtechniques.com
A good all-around resource site for Webmasters.

ZDNet
http://www.zdnet.com
A great all-around site containing everything from product reviews to how-tos.

For Further Reading

Burdman, Jessica R. *Collaborative Web Development: Strategies and Best Practices for Web Teams.* Redding, MA: Addison Wesley, 1999.

Fleming, Jennifer. *Web Navigation: Designing the User Experience.* Sebastopol, CA: O'Reilly & Associates, 1998.

Greenspun, Philip. *Philip and Alex's Guide to Web Publishing.* San Francisco: Morgan Kaufmann Publishers, Inc., 1999.

Niederst, Jennifer, and Richard Korman. *Web Design in a Nutshell: A Desktop Quick Reference.* Sebastopol, CA: O'Reilly & Associates, 1999.

Nielsen, Jakob. *Designing Web Usability: The Practice of Simplicity.* Indianapolis, IN: New Riders Publishing, 2000.

Powell, Thomas A. *Web Design: The Complete Reference.* Berkeley, CA: Osborne/McGraw-Hill, 2000.

MAGAZINES

Business 2.0
http://www.business2.com

Computer Arts
http://www.computerarts.co.uk

FastCompany
http://www.fastcompany.com

Red Herring
http://www.redherring.com

Wired
http://www.wired.com/wired

Yahoo! Internet Life
http://www.zdnet.com/yil

Index

ABOUT THE AUTHOR

Christopher D. Goranson is the founder of ROW14 Web Design House and is also the IT project manager for Pacific Western Technologies, Ltd. He is active in the Web design and GIS community, recently completing a term as president of the Rocky Mountain chapter of the Urban and Regional Information Systems Association. Goranson has a B.A. in economics and currently resides in Denver, Colorado.

PHOTO CREDITS

Cover by Ira Fox; pp. 8, 16, 39 by Ira Fox; p. 13 © www.buy.com; p. 22 © www.guru.com; p. 29 © *Minority Business Entrepreneur* magazine; p. 30 © www.G*Barter.com; p. 32 by Maura Burochow; p. 34 © www.bn.com; p. 37 © VolunteerMatch.org; pp. 41, 43 © Yahoo!Geocities.com; p. 47 © FreeMerchant.com.

SERIES DESIGN

Les Kanturek

LAYOUT

Geri Giordano